TRACKING DOWN

THE
ROMANS
IN BRITAIN

D1099932

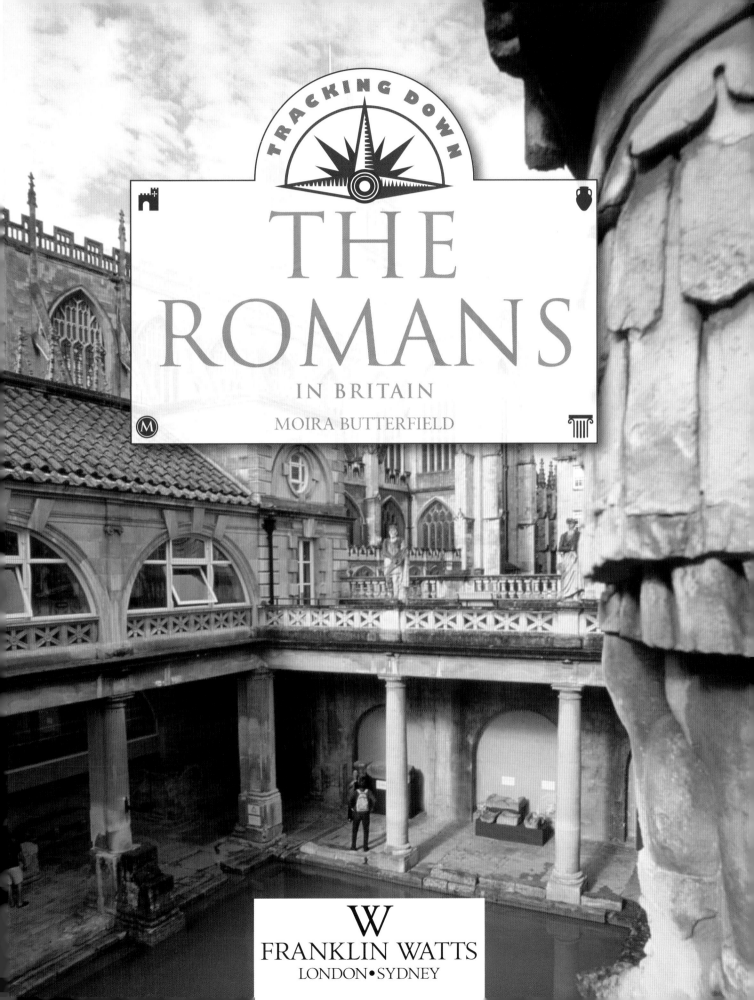

TRACKING DOWN

THE ROMANS

IN BRITAIN

MOIRA BUTTERFIELD

W

FRANKLIN WATTS
LONDON•SYDNEY

This edition published in 2013 by Franklin Watts

Copyright © 2013 Franklin Watts

Franklin Watts
338 Euston Road
London NW1 3BH

Franklin Watts Australia
Level 17/207 Kent Street
Sydney, NSW 2000

A CIP catalogue record for this book is available
from the British Library.

Dewey number: 936.1'04

ISBN 978 1 4451 1657 0

Printed in China

Franklin Watts is a division of Hachette Children's Books,
an Hachette UK company.

www.hachette.co.uk

Editor: Sarah Ridley
Design: John Christopher/White Design
Editor in Chief: John C. Miles
Art director: Jonathan Hair

Picture credits:
Stefano Amantini/Corbis: front cover. Ancient Art & Architecture Collection: 14bl, 23bl, 28. The Trustees of the British Museum: 17b. Cheshire West and Chester Council: 21tr. Colchester Castle Museum/Colchester & Ipswich Museums: 14cr. Derek Croucher/National Trust PL: 22. Curved-Light/Alamy: 13bl. Derry Drabbs/Alamy: 12. Peter Dunn, English Heritage Graphics Team/English Heritage Photo Library: 20. Steven Fruitsmaak/wikipedia commons: 17t. Alan Gallery/Alamy: 13tr. Scott Heppell/AP/PAI: 16. Holmes Garden Photos/Alamy: 4, 6, 7c, 27. David Martyn Hughes/Alamy: 26tr. Linda Kennedy/Alamy: 21b, 25t. Chris Laurens/Alamy: 26bl. Philippa Lewis/Corbis: 19tr. The London Art Archive/Alamy: 7bl. Museum of London: 5t, 5bl, 10, 11t, 11b. National Museum Wales: 9t. National Trust PL: 23tr. Picturepoint/Topham: 5br. The Print Collector/Alamy: 19bl. Roman Baths Museum Bath/Bath & North East Somerset Council: 18t, 18b. Roman Legionary Museum/National Museum Wales: 8b, 9b. Rolf Richardson/Alamy: 24. Nik Wheeler/Alamy: 15. Richard White: 25b. *Every attempt has been made to clear copyright. Should there be any inadvertent omission please apply to the publisher for rectification.*

CONTENTS

ROMANS IN BRITAIN

Nearly 2,000 years ago, in 43CE, a Roman army arrived to conquer the island they called Britannia – modern day Britain. The Roman Empire wanted to mine Britain's valuable minerals, such as tin, gold and lead. But first, the army had to fight the Celtic tribes who already ruled the land.

↓ People dressed as soldiers at an historical re-enactment. Roman soldiers were well-trained, with more armour and weaponry than the Celts.

The Romans arrive

The Romans first arrived with a small force in 55BCE but they were soon attacked by Celts, and decided not to stay. They came back in 43CE with a much bigger army of about 50,000 men. They landed in Kent and fought their way across south-eastern Britain. Some local kings agreed to Roman rule. Others fought to the death, but eventually the southern half of Britain became a province of Rome, ruled by a Roman governor backed up by the army.

Britain goes part-Roman

It took many years of fighting to make the Roman part of Britain peaceful. But gradually people in the south, east and west began to live a more Roman style of life. The Romans built forts, towns and roads across this part of the country, but they never conquered Scotland or Ireland.

Roman Treasures

⬆ A brooch made of bronze and copper, showing the figure of a running dog. It was made in London in the 2nd century CE.

The Romans left behind lots of remains that you can still see today all over Britain, including stone buildings and objects of all kinds brought to Britain from other parts of their empire. The pre-Roman Celts have left far less, as they led simpler lives and their huts were made of natural materials that have not survived.

⬅ Romans worshipped many gods. This beautiful sculpture of Serapis, the Egyptian god of the underworld, was found in the Temple of Mithras in London (see pages 12-13).

The end of the Empire

From about 250CE, foreign enemies began to attack Roman Britain. The attackers came mainly from areas which are now part of Germany. Eventually enemy forces threatened the whole of the Roman Empire, and the army was called away from Britain in 400CE to try to save Rome itself. Britain was abandoned, and the local rulers had to try to defend themselves without Roman soldiers to help.

⬇ This map shows Roman Britain in about 160CE. Roman engineers built a network of roads that connected towns and cities (see pages 14-15).

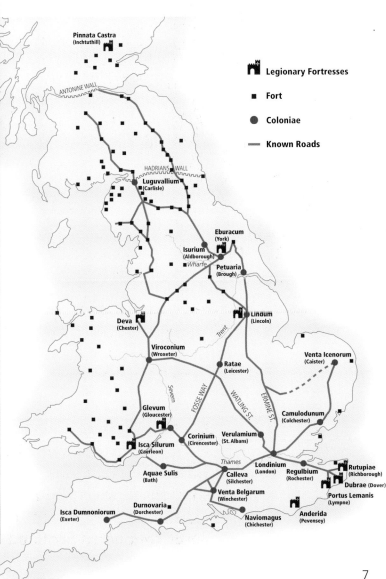

Legend:
- 🏰 Legionary Fortresses
- ■ Fort
- ● Coloniae
- — Known Roads

Pinnata Castra (Inchtuthill)

ANTONINE WALL

HADRIANS WALL

Luguvallium (Carlisle)

Eburacum (York)

Isurium (Aldborough)

Wharfe

Petuaria (Brough)

Deva (Chester)

Lindum (Lincoln)

Viroconium (Wroxeter)

Trent

Ratae (Leicester)

Venta Icenorum (Caister)

Glevum (Gloucester)

Severn

FOSSE WAY

WATLING ST.

ERMINE ST.

Camulodunum (Colchester)

Corinium (Cirencester)

Verulamium (St. Albans)

Isca Silurum (Caerleon)

Thames

Londinium (London)

Regulbium (Rochester)

Rutupiae (Richborough)

Aquae Sulis (Bath)

Calleva (Silchester)

Dubrae (Dover)

Venta Belgarum (Winchester)

Portus Lemanis (Lympne)

Isca Dumnoniorum (Exeter)

Durnovaria (Dorchester)

Naviomagus (Chichester)

Anderida (Pevensey)

The Roman Empire was based in Rome, in Italy. Britannia became a province of the Empire – a region with its own government and army posts. The Romans who arrived were mainly connected to the military or to government. Local people who lived under the Romans are called the Romano-British.

The Roman army

The Roman army was organised into groups of soldiers called legions. Four legions came over to Britain, made up of soldiers who were Roman citizens. Each legion had commanders, officers, foot soldiers (called legionaries) and people with special skills, such as doctors and architects. Auxiliaries also helped invade. They were soldiers who were not born in Italy and so were not Roman citizens. They were often soldiers on horseback.

⬇ These historical re-enactors are marching along like a Roman legion, with a commanding officer at the front and legionaries behind.

The Romano-British

Local people who lived in Britannia soon became 'romanised', which means they began living like Romans. They would have worn Roman clothing, eaten Roman-style food and used Latin, the Roman language. British tribal leaders who helped Rome to rule were rewarded with money and power. These wealthy Romano-British families built grand country villas and town houses in the Roman style.

→ A coin showing the head of Emperor Tiberius, who ruled from 14 to 36CE.

GO VISIT

Local Museum Collections

Archaeologists continue to find Roman remains. Many of these are on display in museums around the country. Here are some of the most typical finds:

Roman coins: the Romans often dropped coins, just like we do today. The coins are decorated with pictures of Roman emperors.

Pottery: broken pottery often turns up in the ground when remains are dug up. Experts can recognise pieces of Roman pot.

Inscriptions: the Romans carved inscriptions (dates and names) on their buildings, in Latin.

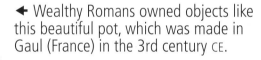

← Wealthy Romans owned objects like this beautiful pot, which was made in Gaul (France) in the 3rd century CE.

Roman slaves

Every Roman household had slaves who did the daily work, such as the cooking and cleaning. Slaves would have worked the farms around Roman villas, and also worked in terrible conditions in the mines dotted around Britain. A Roman slave might be a captive prisoner from a defeated country, or come from a long line of slaves. Slaves had no rights and could be bought and sold by their owners.

A Roman legion could contain up to 6,000 men, and needed a big headquarters, just like a regiment in the modern army. One of the main army bases in Roman Britain was Isca in South Wales. Today it is called Caerleon.

Conquering rebels

Isca was the headquarters of the *Legio II Augusta*, Latin for the Second Augustan Legion. The Romans built the fort in 74/75CE, and stayed there for over 200 years. They first arrived to fight rebellious tribes in Wales. It took 30 years for them to conquer the rebels. Once Wales was peaceful, soldiers were sent from Isca to different parts of the country. Some of them went to help build Hadrian's Wall (see pages 18-19).

➜ There are Roman legionary tombstones at Caerleon, including this one.

How did Isca look?

The Roman name for a fort was a 'castra'. Like other fortresses dotted around the Roman Empire, Isca had everything that its soldiers needed. There were barracks, offices, workshops, stores, a hospital and public baths. A ditch and ramparts (walls) were built around it, with watchtowers for the guards on duty. Outside the walls there was an amphitheatre for entertainment (see pages 22-23), and a settlement for wives and families. Archaeologists have found the remains of the baths, the amphitheatre, the barracks and even the site of the soldiers' toilets.

⬆ This reconstruction of a Roman fort shows the soldiers' barracks inside the walls.

GO VISIT

National Roman Legion Museum, Caerleon

You can visit the remains of the amphitheatre, baths and barracks at Caerleon, and lots of objects found on the site are on display at the National Roman Legion Museum in the town. Look out for a collection of beautiful gemstones with tiny pictures of gods and goddesses carved on them.

Life in Isca

When legionaries weren't out patrolling the countryside they would train or relax off-duty. They might exercise and get clean at the baths, which was the Roman equivalent of a modern sports centre. It had various rooms kept cold, warm or hot like a sauna (see pages 20-21), a big outdoor swimming pool and an exercise hall. For entertainment, the soldiers could go to the amphitheatre to see gladiator fights, animal hunts and the execution of criminals.

⬅ This cornelian gemstone from Caerleon shows the goddess Roma.

BUSY LONDINIUM

Soon after they landed in southern England, the Romans built a wooden bridge over the River Thames. The site around the bridge grew into the busy port and government centre of Londinium, now called London.

Luxury and leaders

The most important official in Roman Britain was the governor, who was based in Londinium just as the Prime Minister is today. The town was a business centre, too. Along the waterfront there were wooden warehouses for storing all sorts of goods, such as wine and olive oil. These were brought by Roman ships from around the Empire. Lining the streets near the river there would have been wooden buildings, housing craftsmen and shopkeepers.

▼ A reconstruction of a Roman wharf at Londinium, where goods from around the Roman Empire arrived by boat up the Thames.

⬆ This selection of Roman coins dating from 65-175CE was found during excavations in Fenchurch Street, London.

GO VISIT

Museum of London

Roman sites in London have long since been built over, but remains sometimes turn up when areas are being dug to prepare for new buildings. Visit the Museum of London to see some of the objects that have been discovered, including marble statues, jewellery and even a pot with Roman face cream preserved inside. The fingerprints of the Roman owner are still in the cream.

Meet me at the forum

Important stone buildings, such as baths and temples, were built in the town. There was a large market square called a forum (near modern-day Gracechurch Street), a basilica (a town hall), a palace for the governor and an amphitheatre (see pages 22-23) as well as a fort for troops. People would gather to chat or to do business in the forum, and sometimes to listen to important announcements. There might have been statues dotted around it, just as in modern town centres.

➤ This statue head of the god Mithras was found in the Temple of Mithras in London.

Temple of Mithras

The remains of a temple dedicated to Mithras were found in 1954. Mithras was a mysterious god of light worshipped by Roman men, especially soldiers. They could only join the secret cult by going through a tough initiation ceremony. They had to stand in a trench and get drenched in the blood of a bull sacrificed above them. The temple remains were moved to a nearby site at Queen Victoria Street, EC4, where they can be visited.

BRITAIN GETS ROADS

Once the Romans had arrived they began to build roads between their forts and towns. It's still possible to walk on a section of original Roman road at Wheeldale in North Yorkshire. It was probably built between two Roman forts, so you would be following in the footsteps of Roman soldiers.

Roads to help Romans

The Romans built over 13,000 km of road in their British province, to make governing the country easier. Up until then, there would only have been rough muddy trackways through the countryside. Proper roads helped soldiers march or ride long distances, and carts full of supplies could reach Roman towns from distant places. Government messages could be sent quickly around the country, too. We know that during Roman times it took roughly three days to ride along a Roman road from Londinium to Caerleon in South Wales (see pages 10-11).

◆ The preserved section of Roman road at Wheeldale. It still has its original stones and drainage ditches.

➔ A Roman milestone at Wheeldale, still standing after more than 1,500 years.

How to build a Roman road

Roman road surveyors would first mark out a route using wooden stakes and measuring instruments to plot a straight line. Wherever they could, they made their roads straight, to avoid hidden corners where travellers could be ambushed by enemies. Soldiers then dug two drainage ditches and built the road surface in the middle, using layers of stones. They made the surface slightly sloped so that water would run off the roadway. Making so many roads by hand must have been tough back-breaking work.

♦ Watling Street in the City of London is on the route of an important Roman road that stretched from the south to the Midlands.

How far to home?

Along their roads the Romans set up milestones, which they engraved or painted with the distance to the next Roman settlement. A Roman mile measured 1,481 metres, which is shorter than a modern mile. At intervals beside the roads there were way stations – houses where government officials could stop on their journeys. There were small roadside inns, too, where ordinary travellers could buy some food and sleep for the night.

GO VISIT

Roman Roads

As well as Wheeldale, there are sections of preserved Roman road you can visit at Blackstone Edge in Yorkshire and Holtye in Sussex. Some modern roads follow the routes of Roman roads, including the Fosse Way, running from Lincoln to Exeter. It is the only example to keep its original Roman name. About 100 Roman milestones still survive in Britain.

SOLDIER'S TOWN

Soon after the Romans arrived they conquered Camulodunum, now called Colchester. It had been the base of a powerful local tribe, but the Romans founded their own town there in 49CE.

Old soldiers arrive

Roman Camulodunum was a military town, built first as a fort and then as a settlement for retired soldiers. Buildings were erected for them to live in, and land was taken from local people and given to the old soldiers to farm. The Romans hoped that by encouraging old soldiers to settle in Britain, the country would eventually become more Roman.

➜ Part of the tombstone of an army cavalryman called Longinus Sdapeze, who came to Britain with the Roman army in about 43CE. He is shown on horseback defeating a tribesman.

➔ The Colchester Vase, decorated with a picture of a fight between two gladiators, called Memnon and Valentinius. Found in Colchester, it is on display at the Colchester Castle Museum.

Romans around town

Roman towns such as Colchester were built in a neat pattern of criss-crossing streets. As well as houses and government buildings there were shops, temples and even a theatre where Romans could enjoy watching plays, singers and dancers. In the middle of Camulodunum there was a massive temple dedicated to the Emperor Claudius. Colchester Castle is built on top of the temple ruins.

GO VISIT

Colchester Castle Museum

Colchester Castle was built in medieval times on the foundations of the Roman Temple of Claudius. It is now a museum packed full of Roman artefacts. You can walk through the temple foundations, and discover the story of Boudica's attack. The displays include the famous Roman tombstones shown on these pages, as well as a beautiful bronze statue of the god Mercury and a stone sphinx with a human head and lion's body, crouching over another head. It was probably a decoration on a tomb.

← This tombstone shows a Roman centurion called Marcus Favonius Facilis. Both this and the tombstone shown on page 16 can be seen at Colchester Castle.

A terrible attack

In 60CE Celtic tribes revolted against the Romans, led by their queen, Boudica. Her forces attacked and destroyed Camulodunum, killing thousands of people. About 200 Roman soldiers tried to hold up inside the Temple of Claudius, but after two days they were killed and the temple was burnt. After Boudica's forces were defeated in 61CE, the town was rebuilt.

HADRIAN'S WALL

In 122CE the Emperor Hadrian visited Britain. He decided to build a wall across northern England to defend his empire from enemy attack. It was dotted with forts and lookout posts manned by soldiers. You can still walk alongside remains of the wall and visit the ruins of some of the forts.

Guarding the border

Legionaries built the wall using stone and turf. It stretched for 117 km, to keep out the Picts, unconquered tribes who lived in Scotland and sometimes raided Roman lands. It was also there to impress local people with Rome's power, and to control who came in and out of Roman territory. There were gates in the forts on the wall, and the soldiers on duty would check on anyone who wanted to pass through from one side to the other.

▼ Parts of Hadrian's Wall survive, stretching across the northern landscape.

On the lookout

At intervals along the wall there were mini forts, big enough for a few dozen troops. Between them there were turrets fit for just a handful of soldiers, who would patrol the wall or keep a lookout. Further back behind the wall there were much larger forts, big enough for hundreds of troops, with barracks, stables, workshops and stores. Riders would have carried messages between the various forts.

➜ Roman toilets at Housesteads Fort on Hadrian's Wall. When they went to the toilet, the soldiers sat together in rows on seats above the trenches on the left and right.

GO VISIT

Hadrian's Wall

You can visit excavated forts such as Housesteads and Vindolanda, to see what life was like for the troops at Hadrian's Wall. At Vindolanda over 1,000 fragments of Roman writing were discovered, the oldest handwritten documents in the country. You can see an exhibition about them, as well as lots of objects such as shoes, jewellery and weaponry found along the wall.

Far from home

The soldiers who manned Hadrian's Wall were auxiliaries, which meant they didn't come from Rome. Some of them would probably have been Britons who joined the Roman army. Among them were cavalry troops, and and there were likely to have been sharp-shooting archers, too. Villages grew up by the forts, where local families lived and where veteran soldiers retired.

◄ The Vindolanda Tablets are letters and notes written on slivers of wood, dating from Roman times.

ROMAN BATHS AND TEMPLES

At Aquae Sulis, now the city of Bath, the Romans built big public baths and a temple to the goddess Sulis Minerva. It was a renowned attraction for Roman visitors.

➤ The gilded bronze head of Sulis Minerva, probably from a statue which once stood inside the sacred temple at Aquae Sulis. You can see it at Bath.

The Sacred Spring

A natural hot water spring bubbles out of the ground at Bath. Because of that it was considered a sacred site, even before Roman times. Both Celts and Romans believed that offerings and messages thrown into the spring would reach the goddess Sulis Minerva, who would then grant wishes. By 75CE the Romans had channelled the hot spring water to run through a series of luxury baths inside grand buildings.

GO VISIT

The Roman Baths

You can visit the Roman Baths at Bath and hear their amazing story. Roman treasures recovered from the baths are on display, including lots of offerings made to the goddess. These include coins, jewellery and curses carved on pieces of lead (such as this one, right). The curse tablets were thrown into the water, to ask the goddess to punish people for stealing or cheating.

A visit to the baths

Aquae Sulis was similar to the public baths built all over the Empire. They were like modern beauty spas. Visitors would wander through a row of warm and hot rooms with underfloor heating, bathing in warm, hot or cold pools as they went. Instead of soap, slaves would rub oil on the bathers' skin and scrape it off with a tool called a strigil, to get rid of dirt. Bathers might sit and chat, play board games or even eat snacks.

➜ The baths are on the site of a thermal spring, and hot water still bubbles up into them from the ground below.

⬇ A carving of a mysterious face, once part of the entrance to the temple. You can see it at the Roman Baths in Bath.

A visit to the temple

The Temple of Sulis Minerva was near the baths. Inside the temple priests kept sacred flames burning and there was a life-sized figure of the goddess. In a dark shadowy chamber worshippers could see the Sacred Spring, looking steamy and magical as it bubbled up. Drinking or bathing in the spring water was thought to heal illness. Outside the temple there were open-air altars for sacrificing animals to the goddess, to please her.

SEE THE SHOW

Chester was an important Roman town called Deva Victrix. It had a big open-air stadium called an amphitheatre, built around 100CE, for staging grisly fights to the death between gladiators.

Keeping the crowd happy

The Romans celebrated lots of religious festivals and public holidays, when they held games in amphitheatres to keep the public entertained. The amphitheatre in Chester could fit in a crowd of up to 8,000 people. Before the show they would have milled around outside, buying snacks and souvenirs. Then they would have entered the round-shaped stadium.

↓ An artist's impression of what Chester's amphitheatre would have looked like in its heyday.

Chilling finds

The amphitheatre had an altar at one end, dedicated to Nemesis, the goddess of punishment. Around the stadium there were dungeons for prisoners. The crowd came to see criminals executed as well as gladiators fighting. In the middle of the amphitheatre archaeologists found some blocks with metal rings on them, probably for chaining up prisoners or animals during the show.

Chester Amphitheatre

You can visit Chester Amphitheatre and discover its story at the Chester Visitor Centre, where you can also see archaeologists at work on finds from the site. Among the remains found are human bones and a human tooth, perhaps from a dead gladiator. You can actually walk in the footsteps of gladiators at the amphitheatres at Caerleon and at Cirencester in Gloucestershire.

➤ A gladiator shown on a Roman mosaic picture. Different types of gladiator had different armour and weaponry. This one is carrying a short sword and a shield.

⬆ The remains of a block used for chaining prisoners or animals in the amphitheatre.

Death show

Gladiators were highly-trained fighters, but they were mainly slaves or battle captives, with no choice but to fight. As well as gladiators, the crowd probably saw acrobats, jugglers, wrestlers and boxers. The boxers wore spiked gloves or gloves weighed down with lead. Archaeologists have found lots of yellow sand in the amphitheatre remains at Chester. It was probably scattered in the ring to soak up blood.

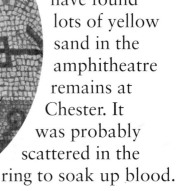

A COUNTRY VILLA

During Roman times most ordinary Britons lived in wooden huts with thatch on the roof. But the richest most important families had stone country houses called villas. One of the grandest was at Chedworth in Gloucestershire, built in the fourth century CE. The remains have been excavated and are now on show to visitors.

Sacred site

Chedworth Villa was near the important Roman town of Corinium (now called Cirencester), and it could have been the home of a powerful local family connected to the town. It would have had farmland around it, worked by slaves belonging to the family. It was built close to a natural spring which was thought to be a sacred place. There was a small shrine built round the spring, where the people from the villa would have made offerings to gods and goddesses. Statues and an altar stood at the shrine.

← The remains of pillars that once held up a grand building at Chedworth.

British-style luxury

Chedworth was shaped like a rectangle. There were rooms on three sides and an entrance at the front, with space in the middle for courtyards. It had over 50 rooms, including baths, dining rooms and lots of underfloor heating for the cold British winters. Expensive mosaics covered the floors and the walls were painted with patterns and pictures. The house even had its own luxury toilet block with freshwater running through it.

➤ The dining room had a fine floor mosaic on the theme of the seasons. This fragment shows the hooded figure of Winter.

GO VISIT

A Roman Villa

At Chedworth Roman Villa you can discover the building remains and some unique finds, including fragments of sacred statues and objects the owners used. Around Roman Britain there are other fine villa sites to visit, including Lullingstone in Kent, Bignor in Sussex and Brading on the Isle of Wight.

➤ A bone hairpin from a number found at Chedworth. The women must have worn their long hair pinned up.

Who lived here?

Chedworth was big enough for quite a few people, but we don't know who lived there. We can guess that they were rich because the villa was so grand. The owners would have feasted in the spacious dining rooms or relaxed in the baths, their every need looked after by slaves. The only Roman name ever found at the villa was the name 'Censorinus', carved onto a silver spoon dating to the mid-4th century.

A MYSTERY PALACE

In 1960 a workman digging a trench made an amazing discovery near Fishbourne in West Sussex. He found rubble that turned out to be the remains of a luxury Roman palace, hidden for centuries underground.

Magnificent mansion

The palace had over 100 rooms, and was very large, more like Buckingham Palace than a country villa such as Chedworth (see pages 24-25). Nobody knows who lived there. It could have been built for the Roman governor of Britain, or perhaps for a local tribal chief. Fire destroyed it in about 300CE and lots of the rubble was taken away, but some of the floor mosaics survived.

↓ A fine floor mosaic from Fishbourne, showing the god Cupid riding on a dolphin.

Luxury Roman-style

No expense was spared to build Fishbourne Palace. Expert mosaic-makers were probably brought in from abroad to lay the floors. Everywhere had underfloor heating, and there were plenty of shady walkways under rows of colonnades (pillars). The spectacular gardens had pools and fountains, terraces and a view of the sea. A building this big would certainly have needed lots of slaves to keep it running.

← Remains of the hypocaust, Fishbourne's luxury underfloor heating system.

GO VISIT

A Roman Garden

You can explore the neat Roman garden at Fishbourne and even see a reconstructed Roman potting shed. The Romans grew flowers, but also herbs used for cooking and for making medicine. For example, they used chamomile and mint for soothing a cold. There is also a Roman garden to visit at Caerleon (see pages 10-11) and at Chesters Fort on Hadrian's Wall (see pages 18-19).

Dinner at Fishbourne

The wealthy people who lived at Fishbourne would have had a comfortable life. They would have eaten the finest food, cooked by slaves in the kitchens over fires and in wood ovens. Guests would have eaten their dinner with spoons and knives but not forks. Roman writers described how people lay on couches around low tables, perhaps being entertained by singers and musicians.

← The peaceful Roman garden at Fishbourne Palace.

ENEMIES FROM THE SEA

The Romans built a string of forts along a stretch of the south coast, to protect their empire from raiders. Regulbium in Kent was one of the first they built. It guarded an important channel that led to the River Thames. Its modern name is Reculver.

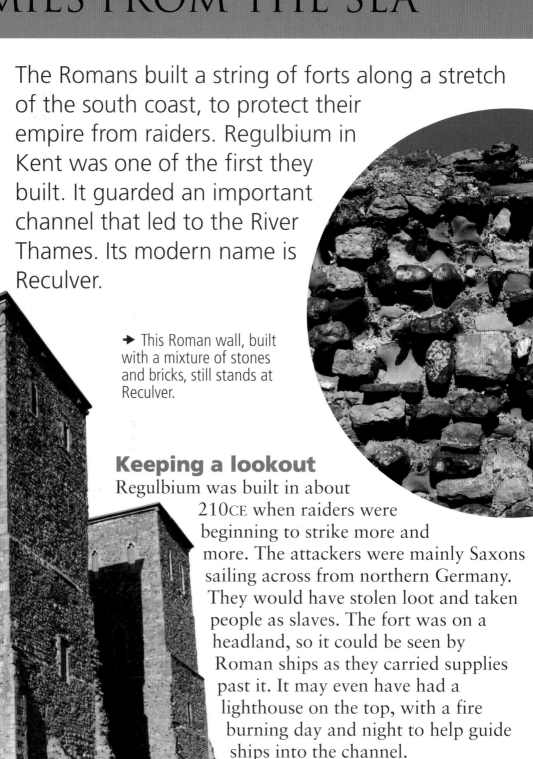

➤ This Roman wall, built with a mixture of stones and bricks, still stands at Reculver.

Keeping a lookout

Regulbium was built in about 210CE when raiders were beginning to strike more and more. The attackers were mainly Saxons sailing across from northern Germany. They would have stolen loot and taken people as slaves. The fort was on a headland, so it could be seen by Roman ships as they carried supplies past it. It may even have had a lighthouse on the top, with a fire burning day and night to help guide ships into the channel.

◄ A church was built over the site of Regulbium; these towers date from the 12th century. The whole site is being destroyed by coastal erosion.

Inside the walls

Roman coastal forts had thick high walls to keep raiders out, along with ditches and earth banks. The soldiers could have stayed safely inside and fired at the enemy from the walls. On the site of Regulbium there are traces of barracks, a bathhouse, a guard post and an army headquarters. Around the fort there would have been huts where local people lived. They would have had to shelter in the fort during an attack.

GO VISIT

Roman coastal forts

The Roman legions left Britain in 400CE, but some of their shore forts were reused and made into castles in later centuries. Porchester Castle in Hampshire and Pevensey Castle in East Sussex are both examples where you can still see the old Roman fort remains. Pevensey is said to be haunted by ghostly Roman soldiers marching through its walls!

➤ Soldiers would have been on guard at Regulbium, ready to fight raiders and protect Roman shipping going towards Londinium. (see pages 12-13).

Soldiers of Regulbium

About 500 soldiers would have lived in the fort. We know from old documents that, for at least part of the time, the troops stationed there were from lower Germany and belonged to an army section called the *Cohors I Baetasiorum* – C.I.B. for short. The letters C.I.B. have been found on building materials around the site. We know that the Roman army had some marines and it's likely they might have been based at some of the British shore forts, too.

29

GLOSSARY

Amphitheatre a stadium for entertainment, including fights to the death between gladiators

Archaeologist a trained expert who digs up buried remains and studies them

Auxiliary a soldier who fought for the Roman army but was not a citizen of Rome. Many auxiliaries fought on horseback

Basilica a Roman town hall

Baths a collection of hot and cold pools and exercise areas used by the Romans for cleanliness and relaxation

BCE Before Common Era/Before Christian Era. Used to show that a date in history falls before 1CE

Boudica Queen of the Iceni, a Celtic tribe from the southeast of England. She led a rebellion against the Romans

Britannia the Roman name for Britain

CE Common Era/Christian Era. Used to show that a date falls after 1CE.

Castra a Roman word for a fort

Celts the name given to the people who lived in Britain before the Romans arrived

Centurion an officer in the Roman army, in charge of legionaries

Colonnade a row of pillars

Emperor the ruler of an empire

Forum a Roman town square

Gladiator a professional fighter who performed in front of a crowd

Hypocaust a Roman underfloor heating system

Imperial something connected to the Roman Emperor, such as the Imperial post

Latin the language of the ancient Romans

Legion a Roman army group of between 5 and 6,000 men, with its own name and badge

Legionary a soldier who was a Roman citizen

Milestone a carved stone marking the distance of one Roman mile along a Roman road

Mithras a god of light worshipped by Roman men, especially soldiers

Mosaic a picture made from hundreds of tiny coloured squares

Picts unconquered tribes living in the area now called Scotland

Romano-British Britons who lived under Roman rule

Sacred something thought to be connected to gods or goddesses, such as a temple or a statue

Saxon Shore the east and south coast of England, where Saxons attacked the Roman Empire

Thermal spring a spring of warm water

Tribe a group of people with the same customs and language

Veteran a retired soldier

Villa a Roman country house with a farm

PLACES TO VISIT

Aquae Sulis
Roman Baths, Abbey Church Yard,
Bath BA1 1LZ
www.romanbaths.co.uk

Arbeia Roman Fort and Museum
Baring Street, South Shields, Tyne and
Wear NE33 2BB
www.twmuseums.org.uk/arbeia.html

Bignor Roman Villa
Bignor, Pulborough, West Sussex
RH20 1PH
www.bignorromanvilla.co.uk.

British Museum
Great Russell Street, London
WC1B 3DG
www.britishmuseum.org

Chedworth Roman Villa
Yanworth, nr Cheltenham,
Gloucestershire
*www.nationaltrust.org.uk/
chedworth-roman-villa/*
There is also an information site at
www.chedworthromanvilla.com

Chesters Roman Fort
Hexham, Northumberland NE46 4EU
*www.english-heritage.org.uk/
daysout/properties/
chesters-roman-fort-and-museum-
hadrians-wall/*

Chester's Roman Amphitheatre
Situated in Grosvenor Park, Grosvenor
Park Road, Chester, Cheshire CH1 1QQ
*www.english-heritage.org.uk/
daysout/properties/chester-roman-
amphitheatre/*

Colchester Castle
Castle Park, Colchester, Essex CO1 1TJ
www.cimuseums.org.uk/home.html

Fishbourne Roman Palace
Salthill Road, Fishbourne, Chichester,
West Sussex PO19 3QR
*http://sussexpast.co.uk/properties-to-
discover/fishbourne-roman-palace*

**Hadrian's Wall
and Housesteads Fort**
Bardon Mill, Hexham,
Northumberland NE47 6NN
www.hadrians-wall.org

Lullingstone Roman Villa
nr Eynsford,
Kent DA4 0JA
*www.english-heritage.org.uk/
daysout/properties/lullingstone-
roman-villa/*

Museum of London
London Wall,
London EC2Y 5HN
www.museumoflondon.org.uk

National Roman Legion Museum
High Street, Caerleon,
Newport,
Wales
NP18 1AE
www.museumwales.ac.uk/en/roman/

**Roman Army
Museum and Vindolanda**
Bardon Mill,
Hexham,
Northumberland NE47 7JN
www.vindolanda.com.
To see all the Vindolanda tablets
online, go to
www.vindolanda.csad.ox.ac.uk

WEBLINKS
www.pbs.org/wgbh/nova/lostempires/roman/
Find Roman recipes, walk round a Roman bath complex and
build a virtual aquaduct.

www.bbc.co.uk/schools/primaryhistory/romans/
Use this BBC Primary History website to learn about the ancient
Romans and their invasion of Britain.

www. roman-empire.net/children/index.html
Click on 'Your Visit to Ancient Rome!' to explore all sorts of
features of Roman life.

Note to parents and teachers
Every effort has been made by the Publishers to ensure
that the websites in this book are suitable for children,
that they are of the highest educational value, and that
they contain no inappropriate or offensive material.
However, because of the nature of the Internet, it is
impossible to guarantee that the contents of these sites
will not be altered. We strongly advise that Internet
access is supervised by a responsible adult.

INDEX